D1064942

OLYSLAGER AUTO LIBRARY

# Armour on Wheels to 1942

compiled by the OLYSLAGER ORGANISATION
edited by Bart H. Vanderveen

FREDERICK WARNE & Co Ltd
London and New York

## THE OLYSLAGER AUTO LIBRARY

This book is one of a growing range of titles on major transport subjects. Titles published so far include:

The Jeep
Cross-Country Cars from 1945
Half-Tracks
Scammell Vehicles
Tank and Transport Vehicles of World War 2
Armour on Wheels to 1942
Fire-Fighting Vehicles
Fire and Crash Tenders from 1950
Earthmoving Vehicles
Wreckers and Recovery Vehicles
Passenger Vehicles 1893–1940
Buses and Coaches from 1940
Fairground and Circus Transport

American Cars of the 1930s
American Cars of the 1940s
American Cars of the 1950s
American Trucks of the Early Thirties
American Trucks of the Late Thirties

British Cars of the Early Thirties
British Cars of the Late Thirties
British Cars of the Early Forties
British Cars of the Late Forties
British Cars of the Early Fifties
British Cars of the Late Fifties

Motorcycles to 1945
Motorcycles and Scooters from 1945



---

Library of Congress Catalog Card No. 78-8058

ISBN 0 7232 1848 X

Filmset and printed in Great Britain
by BAS Printers Limited, Wallop, Hampshire
402·275

# INTRODUCTION

Before the advent of the track-laying combat vehicle which became known as the tank, armoured fighting vehicles were invariably of the wheeled type and usually based on existing passenger car or truck chassis.

When the tank appeared, the wheeled armoured vehicle was by no means ousted. On roads, the latter was very much faster—not to mention quieter and more reliable—and the 'armoured car' was usually employed for different roles: scouting, reconnaissance, supply convoy protection, etc.

After the Great War—or First World War—armoured cars remained in service in many countries for military and police duties.

During the late twenties and throughout the thirties, more sophisticated designs were developed, the rear-engined four-wheel drive type eventually becoming the most numerous. There were also six- and eight-wheelers and semi-track configurations (for which the reader is referred to the title *Half-Tracks* in this series).

At the beginning of the Second World War the British, expecting invasion at any time, produced a mass of improvised types, some of which are included in this selection of some 200 pictures of armoured wheeled vehicles from many countries. The book is subdivided into four parts, *viz*. The Early Years (pages 4–10), The Great War (11–27), The Inter-War Years (28–47) and The *Blitzkrieg* Era (48–63). Additional illustrations from these periods will be found in several other titles in the Olyslager Auto Library, listed on the facing page, and in *The Observer's Army Vehicles Directory—to 1940* and *The Observer's Fighting Vehicles Directory—World War II*.

**Piet Olyslager MSIA MSAE KIVI**

The design for this awesome wheeled combat vehicle reputedly dates from nearly 500 years ago (1480). At the front it featured a battering ram and the machine was rear-driven by six horses. Steering was by a foot-operated yoke, acting on the front axle.

## THE EARLY YEARS

4A Duryea/Davidson

4A: As early as 1898 Colonel Royal P. Davidson of the US Army (at the time he was a Major and working at the Northwestern Military and Naval Academy) designed and built a motor gun carriage which, although fitted only with an armour shield, is considered to be one of the world's first 'armoured cars'. It carried a ·30 calibre Colt machine gun and was based on a three-wheeled Duryea pneumatic-tyred automobile, which afterwards was converted to four wheels, as shown. A similar gun car was built at the same time by Frederick R. Simms in England.

4B: In the year 1900 Davidson built two more armour-clad gun carriages, both based on steam-propelled cars. One of these has survived and is exhibited in the Museum of Science and Industry in Chicago. These vehicles too, carried a Colt automatic machine gun.

4B Davidson steam car

5A Fowler

5A–D : In the South African or Boer War at the beginning of this century the British Army employed several dozen steam traction engines, notably Fowlers, for hauling supplies and guns. In 1900 some armoured units were taken into service together with armoured trailers. With the aid of special channels, field guns could be loaded and carried in these wagons. The traction engines were of Fowler's B5 type ; there were four armoured models.

5B Fowler

5C Fowler

5D Fowler

## THE EARLY YEARS

6A: In 1902 the French firm of Charron, Girardot et Voigt produced this armoured car, which was displayed at the Paris motor show in December of that year. It featured a circular armoured 'tub' on the rear of a contemporary chain-drive 4-cyl. 40 HP CGV car and was armed with a Hotchkiss machine gun. One periodical claimed that the machine saw active service in Transvaal, but this is unlikely.

6A CGV

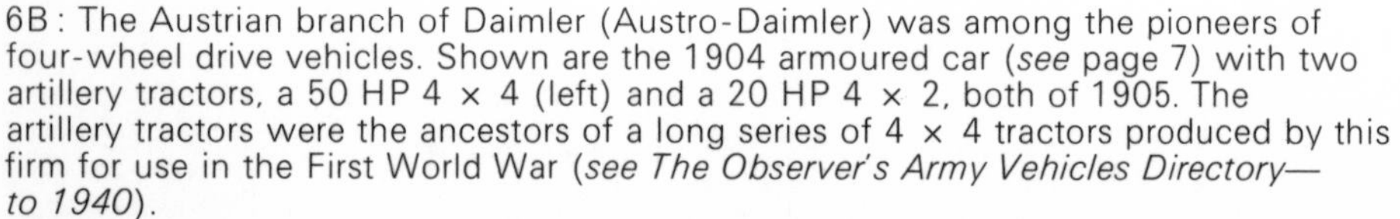

6B: The Austrian branch of Daimler (Austro-Daimler) was among the pioneers of four-wheel drive vehicles. Shown are the 1904 armoured car (*see* page 7) with two artillery tractors, a 50 HP 4 × 4 (left) and a 20 HP 4 × 2, both of 1905. The artillery tractors were the ancestors of a long series of 4 × 4 tractors produced by this firm for use in the First World War (*see The Observer's Army Vehicles Directory—to 1940*).

6B Austro-Daimler

7A/B: The Austro-Daimler four-wheel drive armoured car of 1903/04 was the first purpose-built vehicle of this type. It was well ahead of its time, most other early armoured vehicles being conversions of standard cars or trucks. The enclosed hull was of curved shape and carried a dome-shaped rotating turret, originally with one but later modified with two openings for Maxim water-cooled machine guns. The car never saw active service.

7C: In 1906 the well-known British firm of Armstrong-Whitworth produced this open-top armoured car, on, reputedly, a Wilson-Pilcher car chassis with Wilson epicyclic transmission. Cars of this make had been made in London during 1901–03, after which Sir W. G. Armstrong, Whitworth & Co. Ltd of Newcastle-upon-Tyne took over, until 1907. Noteworthy on the armoured car are the capstan pulley amidships and the reversible sprag underneath.

7A Austro-Daimler

7B Austro-Daimler

7C Armstrong-Whitworth

8A Ehrhardt

8B Ehrhardt

8C Opel-Darracq

8A: At the 7th International Automobile Exhibition in Berlin in 1906 the Düsseldorf firm of Ehrhardt displayed this *Panzer-automobil zur Verfolgung von Luftballons* (armoured car for the pursuit of balloons). It was based on a 60 HP truck chassis with chain drive and could attain a speed of 45 km/h.
8B: This drawing was intended to give the public some idea of the deployment of the 1906 Ehrhardt (8A). Main armament was a 5-cm anti-aircraft gun, mounted high on a pedestal. The hull was made of 3-mm nickel-steel.
8C: Also displayed in 1906 was an armoured command car on a 40 HP Opel-Darracq car chassis, produced by Ing. Emil August Schmidt of Adam Opel's Berlin branch. The original caption of this artist's impression (which was published in 1914) said that it '. . . shows how two German Army officers were pursued by Belgian lancers while reconnoitring in hostile territory'—a rather unlikely statement.

9: The Germans, prior to 1914, produced several types of self-propelled anti-aircraft/balloon guns. This 5·7-cm type (Krupp L/30) was based on a partly-armoured four-wheel drive Daimler chassis. It appeared in 1909 and the gun was placed in a rotating mounting.

9 Daimler/Krupp

## THE EARLY YEARS



10A: The famous French armaments firm of Hotchkiss brought out their first armoured car in early 1909. Basically it was similar in design to the CGV of 1902 (*see* Fig. 6A) but, logically, somewhat more modern. It carried a Hotchkiss machine gun with armour shield. Four of these cars, known as *Automitrailleuse*, were supplied to Constantinople where they were used in the ensuing Young Turk revolution, first by and subsequently against the Sultan of Turkey.

10B: *Automitragliatrice Isotta Fraschini forza 40 HP* was the name of this 3-ton Italian armoured car, designed in 1911 by Ing. Cattaneo. It carried two machine guns, one of which was mounted in a fully-rotating turret. The shape and general layout of this machine came to be regarded as conventional for many years to come.

10C: This *Autoblindata* was built by the Turin Artillery Arsenal in 1912 on a Fiat truck chassis. It was the first armoured car to be used in the Italo-Turkish War in Tripolitania, Libya, and carried a Maxim machine gun in a searchlight-equipped rotating turret.

10A Hotchkiss

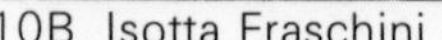

10B Isotta Fraschini

10C Fiat

11A Minerva

11A: Most common of the various types of armoured cars used by the Belgian Army in the Great War—later to be known as the First World War—was the Minerva. This vehicle consisted of a box-shaped hull on a Minerva car chassis, powered by a 4-cyl. Knight-type sleeve-valve engine and fitted with dual rear tyres. Usually a Hotchkiss machine gun was carried but some had a 37-mm gun instead. Some remained in service until the thirties.

11B: Another Belgian *Automitrailleuse* was the SAVA, the chassis for which was made by an Antwerp firm which was later—in 1923—absorbed by Minerva. The SAVA featured a dome-shape open-back rotating turret with one Hotchkiss machine gun. One is shown here on the battlefield near Ypres.

11C: Made in Britain for the Belgian Army in 1915 were these Sheffield-Simplex armoured cars. They were produced in Hayes, Middlesex, to Belgian specifications, on new 6-cyl. 30 HP car chassis supplied by the Sheffield-Simplex Motor Works Ltd of Tinsley near Sheffield.

11B SAVA

11C Sheffield-Simplex

12A: In addition to their Minerva and SAVA armoured cars the Belgians mounted armoured hulls on other touring car chassis, including French Peugeot and Mors, examples of which are shown here.

12B: Peugeot car chassis were also used for armoured cars in their country of origin—France. This photo shows two prototypes, based on the Model 153 12 HP chassis (which was produced in the firm's Audincourt factory during 1913–16 and powered by a 2614-cc engine). Later Peugeot armoured cars were heavier, better armoured, and fitted with wire-spoke wheels, dual rear. The leading car is a standard Model 153 *Torpedo* of 1914.

12A Peugeot, Mors

12B Peugeot

13A Renault

13B Renault

13C White

13A: The French forces used various types of Renault armoured cars. This is an early type which, although having the radiator behind the engine, had the air intake right at front.

13B: Later Renaults, in *Automitrailleuse* (shown) and *Autocanon* (37-mm gun) variants, differed from the earlier design (13A) in several respects. The air intake consisted of horizontal armoured louvres immediately in front of the dash-mounted radiator. This picture was taken on the Somme front in 1916.

13C: To augment the supply of motor vehicles from their own industry the French imported considerable quantities of truck chassis from the United States, e.g. Jeffery, Kelly-Springfield, Packard, Pierce-Arrow and White. Of the latter make, several hundred chassis were used as the basis for armoured cars; these became the most numerous *Automitrailleuse* of the French Army and many remained in service until the Second World War, albeit in modified form. Shown is one of the original pattern in use in 1923 in the German Ruhr area.

# THE GREAT WAR

14A Armoured 3-wheeler

14A: The British armed forces in 1914 used a variety of armoured vehicles, mostly of the improvised type. Shown is a rare three-wheeled machine, based on a motorcycle.

14B AC

14B: AC Cars Ltd of Thames Ditton, Surrey, in 1915 produced this experimental light armoured car on a strengthened version of their contemporary car chassis. Extensive tests by the Army proved that the vehicle was—not surprisingly—unstable and overweight.

14C: To meet requirements for armoured cars in India—for use on the North-West frontier and for internal security duties—a number of car chassis were fitted with improvised armoured hulls. This work was carried out by Indian Railway workshops. The example shown was based on a Standard chassis.

14D: In 1914 the British RNAS (Royal Naval Air Service) aeroplane service in France used several locally-armoured cars, one of which, a Talbot-based unit, is illustrated.

14C Standard

14D Talbot

15A: A Rolls-Royce Silver Ghost-based improvised armoured car of the first RNAS pattern, 1914.

15B: This Rolls-Royce, of the first Admiralty pattern—featuring dual rear tyres—was modified in France and fitted with pyramid-shaped overhead armour. It towed a 3-pounder naval gun on a special dual-tyred carriage.

15A Rolls-Royce

15B Rolls-Royce

15D/E: Armoured Car, Rolls-Royce (1914 Admiralty Turreted Pattern) in its final production form weighed 3·5 tons, carried a crew of three and one Vickers-Maxim machine gun. The armour was 8 mm thick and the maximum speed was about 50 mph. After the war they were supplemented by revised editions—the 1920 and 1924 patterns.

15C: Another Rolls-Royce—one of the earliest of its type to be used in France. The 40/50 Silver Ghost chassis, fitted with dual rear tyres, was found to be the most suitable for armoured cars and became the most widely used of the First World War.

15C Rolls-Royce

15D Rolls-Royce

15E Rolls-Royce

# THE GREAT WAR

16A Lanchester

16B Lanchester

16C Austin

16A: Another famous British armoured car was the Lanchester. This was a rather unorthodox machine, with cantilever front and rear springing. Shown is the prototype of late 1914.
16B: A number of Lanchester production models, which featured mudguards, additional front coil springs and other improvements, were used in Russia in 1916/17. Some are shown here on the Russian front in Galicia. They performed exceptionally well.

16C/D: The Austin Motor Co. produced some 480 armoured cars on a modification of their 30 HP Colonial chassis. Until 1917 they were supplied almost exclusively to the Imperial Russian Government (*see* page 21). A distinguishing feature was their twin cylindrical machine gun turrets, side by side, in the base of which spare tyres were carried. There was a duplicate steering system at the rear and the shape of the hull was modified several times. Late production models had dual rear tyres.

16D Austin

17A Austin

17A: Austin armoured cars, being so numerous, were in many instances captured and employed by the opposite side, e.g. the Austrians and Germans.

17C Leyland

17B AEC

17B: AEC B-type armoured car of 1915. This experimental heavy vehicle was based on the solid-tyred chassis normally used for LGOC buses and was one of the first of the War Office—most armoured cars at this time being the responsibility of the Admiralty.

17C: The RAF-type Leyland chassis also appeared with armoured bodywork. Four were made in 1915 for use in German East Africa. They are shown here at the main entrance of the makers' works at Leyland, Lancs.

17D: A batch of armoured cars produced in 1915 by Wolseley Motors Ltd on imported American Pierce-Arrow truck chassis for use by the Royal Marine Artillery Anti-Aircraft Brigade. Most of these vehicles were armed with a Vickers Naval 2-pdr 'pom pom' gun.

17D Pierce-Arrow/Wolseley

18A–C: Canada's first armoured fighting vehicles were these open-topped machine gun carriers, produced in 1914 in the USA on Autocar truck chassis. They came to England in October 1914 with what became known as the 1st Canadian Motor Machine Gun Brigade and from 1915 to 1918 twenty of them saw active service with the Canadian Contingent in France. The vehicle shown in Fig. 18B is on display in the Canadian War Museum in Ottawa.

18B Autocar

18A Autocar

18C Autocar

19A: This Italian armoured car consisted of an armoured body by Ansaldo on the popular Lancia Model 1Z truck chassis. Unusual was the small turret on top of the main turret; the smaller carried one, the larger two machine guns. It was Italy's most important armoured car at the time and captured specimens were employed by the Germans. The twin rails over the front, ending in wire cutters, enabled the vehicle to cope with wire obstacles stretched across its path. Note the armour-plate shields protecting the (pneumatic) tyres.

19A Lancia/Ansaldo

19B Isotta Fraschini/Jarrott

19C Isotta Fraschini/Jarrott

19B/C: A multi-national vehicle was this impressive 100-bhp armoured car. It was designed in the autumn of 1914 for the Russian Imperial Government by Englishman Charles Jarrott on a 100–120-bhp Italian Isotta Fraschini car chassis. The constructional work was carried out by Messrs Barker of London, the armour-plating being supplied by Vickers Ltd. In general appearance it was not unlike the Isotta Fraschini armoured car of 1911 (*see* 10B).

## THE GREAT WAR

20A/B : This armoured car was reputedly designed and built in 1915 by two Russian comrades-in-arms : André Larsky and Frederick Eberhardt.

20A Larsky-Eberhardt

20B Larsky-Eberhardt

20C Renault/Mgebrow

20C : Most armoured vehicles employed by the Imperial Russian Army were imported from Western Europe, either complete or in chassis form. This unit was produced in Russia in 1915 on a French Renault chassis and was known as the Renault/Mgebrow. It is shown being captured by German troops in Livonia.

20D : Russian heavy armoured car on American Packard truck chassis. A Vickers quick-firing 40-mm automatic gun was carried in a rotating open-back turret. Picture shows the vehicle after capture by the Germans.

20D Packard

21A: The Russians used large numbers of British Austin armoured cars. These—'Valiant' and 'Gallant'—are of the earliest pattern, which had a rather high cab roof, limiting the forward traverse of the machine guns (later production had a lower cab with sloping front and vertical sides). They also had solid studded rubber tyres.

21B Austin

21B: During the 50th anniversary of the 1917 Revolution the Soviet Army paraded a number of replicas of the Austin veterans—mock-ups on modern truck chassis. BMC lost no time in publicizing 'the durability of Austin products'. . .

21C: Later batches of the early Austins had pneumatic tyres of two types, both shown here. The right-hand front tyre is of the 'KT' type with studded tread (*see* also page 16).

21A Austin

21C Austin

22A Mercedes

22B Mercedes

22A: As early as 1904 there had been an armour-clad Daimler car and shown here is a *c.* 1914 Mercedes with armour-plating, also from the Daimler Motoren Gesellschaft of Stuttgart-Untertürkheim.
22B: This partly armoured 60 HP Mercedes car was captured from the Germans and subsequently used by the French headquarters staff in Paris in October 1914.

22D Büssing

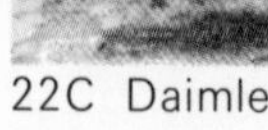

22C Daimler

22C: In 1915 Daimler produced a four-wheel-drive 9-ton *Panzerwagen*, which had dual driving controls, front and rear. The power unit was an 80 HP 4-cyl. petrol unit of just under 10 litres cubic capacity.

22D: Heinrich Büssing at Braunschweig (Brunswick) also built a big four-wheel drive armoured car in 1915. It was powered by a 100 HP 6-cyl. engine. Only one was produced.

23A Ehrhardt

23B: German Mannesmann-Mulag truck chassis with armoured bodywork of *c.* 1916. This vehicle can best be described as an armoured personnel and supply carrier. It carried powerful spotlights at front and rear.

23C: Another truck-based armoured vehicle was the Junovic PA1 *Strassenpanzer* of the Austro-Hungarian Army. Three of these were built, on Austro-Daimler and/or Praga chassis. Shown is a Type B, which unlike the Type A was fitted with a spotlight. It carried a crew of five and two machine guns.

23A: In addition to the one-off Daimler and Büssing armoured cars (*see* previous page), Ehrhardt in 1915 also produced an armoured car. Of the Ehrhardt, however, an improved version went into production in 1917 and 12 were made. Two of these are shown here, as part of a *Panzerkraftwagen-Maschinengewehrzug*, which also comprised one staff car, two GS trucks and a mobile workshop. The 1917 Ehrhardt weighed 7750 kg (*v.* 9500 kg for the 1915 model).

23B Mannesmann-Mulag

23C Junovic

# An Armored Truck with Revolving Gun-Turret

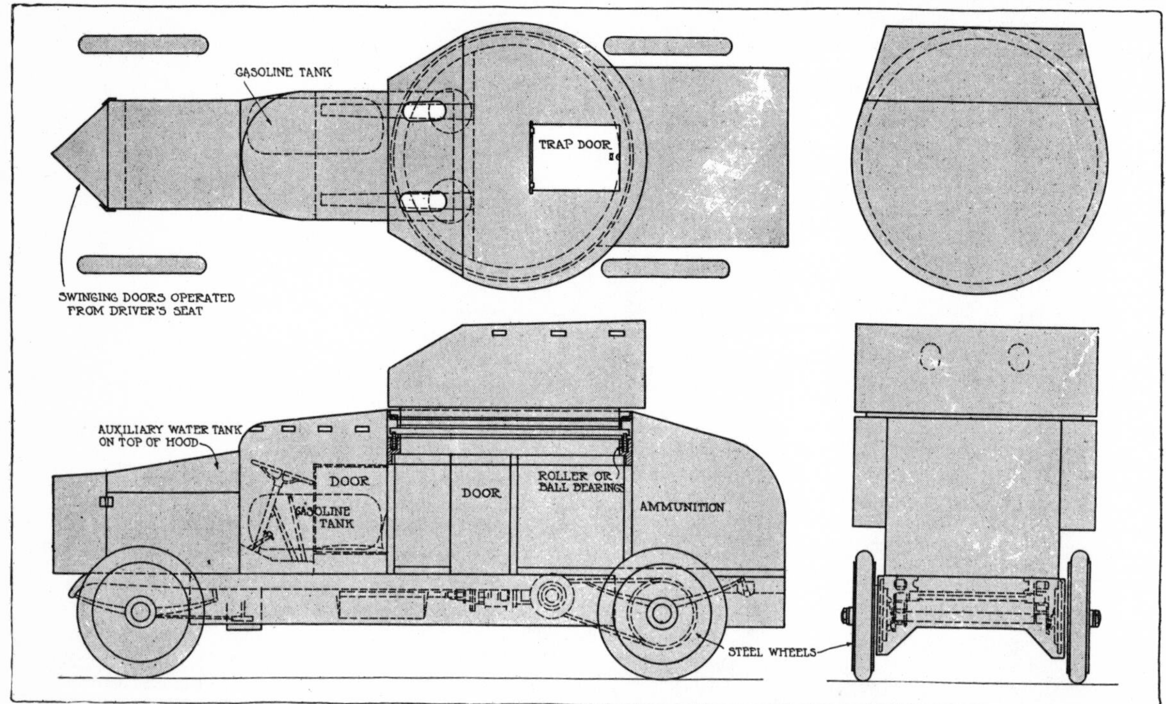


*As reported in* The Automobile *for November 19, the Armored Motor Car Corp. has been organized and incorporated in New York City for the purpose of producing an armored truck mounting two machine guns in a revolving turret. The illustration gives a side elevation, plan and rear views of the truck and a plan of the turret, showing the various constructional features.*

*J. H. Allen, organizer of the concern, has a patent pending covering the application of a revolving turret to a motor truck. The steel bodies will be built on contract and mounted on 2-ton Federal chassis. The two guns which are to be mounted will probably be Maxims firing 600 shots per minute.*

*Mr. Allen, in speaking of the field for such an armored truck, pointed out that under modern war conditions cavalry forces are practically useless for actual work on the battlefield or in reconnoitering under fire, as they are unable to withstand the terrible effects of high-power artillery and rifles. On the other hand, an armored car could not only pass practically unscathed through a withering rain of rifle bullets, etc., but could also do great execution with its machine guns. The revolving feature of the turret permits the fire of these guns to be directed against the enemy, irrespective of the direction in which the truck is traveling. The radiator is protected by swinging doors of armor plate.*

24A Federal

24A: In November 1914 the American journal, *The Automobile*, published this drawing and description of a Federal truck-based armoured car.

24B: During 1917–18, the years when the United States actively took part in the First World War, the US Army employed large numbers of 1-ton White trucks (as well as heavier types). In 1917 one of these chassis was used as the basis for an experimental armoured car, albeit fitted with a special engine and rear axle. Known as M1917 it carried a crew of four and one machine gun.

24B White

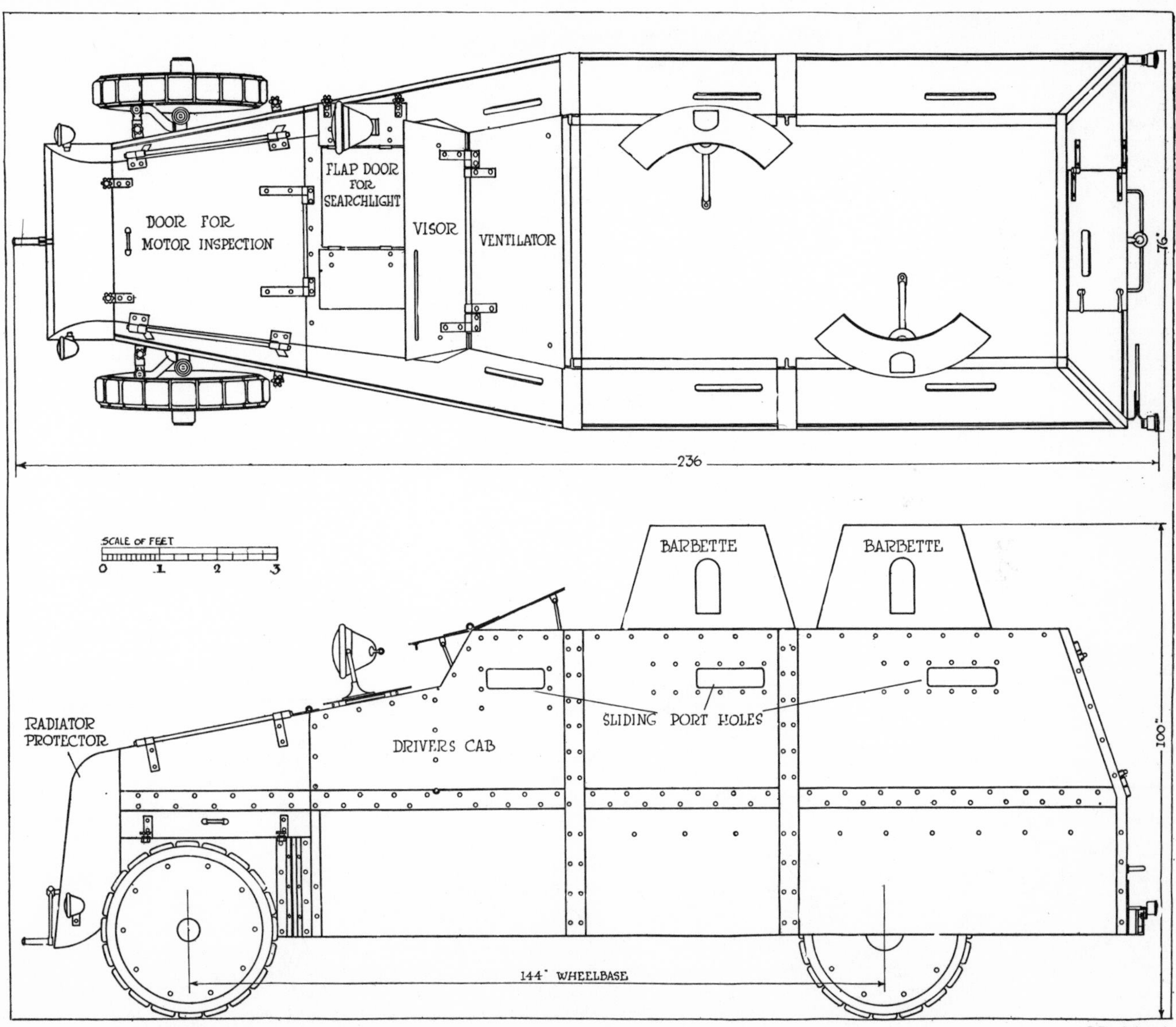


25: In 1916 the 1st Armored Motor Battery of the New York National Guard was equipped with three armoured cars, built on Mack AC, Riker (Locomobile) and White truck chassis and financed by a group of wealthy and patriotic New Yorkers. The armoured hulls were made by the Carnegie Steel Corp. and the vehicles were employed in the Mexican border conflict. Later, when the US had entered the European war, they appeared in parades and 'Uncle Sam Needs You' recruitment campaigns. Shown are a plan and side elevation of the vehicle, which weighed 9052 lb.

25 Mack

26A Olympian

26A: Some strange vehicles saw the light of day, exemplified by this Olympian. It was possibly a training vehicle, the 'armour' plating looking suspiciously thin. Cars and trucks of this marque were made only during 1917–21, by Olympian Motors Co. of Pontiac, Michigan.

26B: Another early American armoured car was this model built by The Pathfinder Co., a short-lived firm located in Indianapolis, Indiana (1916–18).

26B Pathfinder

26C Jeffery

26C: The Jeffery 'Quad', a 2-ton 4 × 4 four-wheel steer chassis, was produced in large numbers by the Thomas B. Jeffery Co. (later Nash) of Kenosha, Wisconsin. In addition to trucks, several armoured cars appeared on this chassis, from 1914. One of the first models is shown.

27A Jeffery

27C Jeffery/Russell

27A: In 1915 Jeffery brought out 'the first reversible military truck (chassis) to be constructed in America' and the first of these was shipped to London 'to be demonstrated to the military officials of the Allies'. Basically it was a stock 'Quad', but with driving controls at either end. Reverse gear in the 3-speed transmission was substituted by a fourth speed and an independent reverse gear added, giving four speeds forward and reverse. Speed in either direction was 35 mph. It was used for armoured cars of various types.

27B Jeffery

27B: Jeffery armoured car of the type used by the US Army on the Mexican border in 1916. It featured a rather large hull with two turrets, one in the centre and one below at the rear.

27C: The Canadian-built Russell Armoured Truck of 1915 was based on the Jeffery 'reversible Quad' chassis with four-wheel steering and dual controls. Forty were made and shipped to the UK. The hull consisted of double $\frac{1}{4}$-in armour-plating with 1-in spacing. Illustrated is the rear end of the vehicle, opened up to show the rear steersman's position.

## THE INTER-WAR YEARS

28A Heigl

28B: Belgian Minerva armoured car in 1933. This was a modernized version of the widely-used 1914 Minerva (*see* 11A). At about this time these veterans were beginning to be replaced by modern French Berliet armoured cars with four-wheel drive.

28B Minerva

28A: Following the 1918 Armistice and the collapse of the *Donaumonarchie*, Austria, like Germany, was allowed only a limited number of armoured cars, mainly for police use and training. This improvised *Übungs-Strassenpanzer*, based on a truck chassis, was designed in 1926 by Dr Fritz Heigl, the originator of the authoritative *Taschenbuch der Tanks* (tank pocket guide).

28C Renault

28C: Renault, between the wars, produced several types of armoured cars, as did Berliet and Laffly. This is a Renault *Automitrailleuse* of 1932, based on a modified commercial truck chassis with 70-bhp 4-cyl. engine and rear-wheel drive. On the same chassis existed an armoured personnel carrier.

29C: Larger German dummy armoured cars were based on Adler car chassis, a number of which are shown here during manoeuvres in the early thirties. Later editions of these training vehicles were built on Opel P4 light car chassis (1937–38). They were known also as *Panzer-Nachbildung* (tank imitation).

29C Adler

29D: Some of the Adler Standard 6 chassis were provided with real armoured hulls in 1932/33: the *Kfz. 13* with machine gun (shown) and the *Kfz. 14* with radio equipment. The hulls were made by Daimler-Benz in their Berlin-Marienfelde works. These vehicles were used until the early years of the Second World War.

29B Dixi

29A Dixi

29A/B: The Germans, like the Austrians, were forbidden, under the Treaty of Versailles, to have armoured vehicles for military use, so, to train their *Reichswehr* they used dummies (*Panzerattrappen*) while a new *Panzertruppe* was secretly built up and trained in Russia. Shown is an 'exploded view' (29A) of a plywood and canvas dummy tank; based on a Dixi 3/15 PS light car of the late twenties (29B). This Dixi was produced during 1927–29 under British Austin licence and then continued by BMW until 1931, following the take-over of the Dixi Automobilwerke AG in Eisenach by BMW.

29D Adler

## THE INTER-WAR YEARS

30A: The famous British RAF-type Crossley 'Tender', which had been made in considerable quantities during the Great War, remained in use for many years. A number of them went to Ireland, for police use, and some of these were fitted with metal plates for crew protection.
30B: In 1923 Crossley introduced a purpose-built armoured car, mainly for use in India. However, cars of this type also went to South Africa, Japan and Argentina. This picture was taken in Buenos Aires in July 1928.

30A Crossley

30B Crossley

30C Rolls-Royce

30C: Production of the well-known WWI-type Rolls-Royce armoured cars (*see* page 15) was continued, albeit with various improvements. This is one of the 1920 pattern, fitted with experimental rear wheels. A number of the hulls of these cars were in 1940 placed on Ford V8 truck chassis.

30D: During the 1920s the Indian Government acquired various types of armoured cars built in Britain to their own specification. This was the first—known as 'Armoured Car, Rolls-Royce, 1921 Indian Pattern'. Based on the 40/50 HP Silver Ghost chassis, the hull was similar to that of the somewhat later Crossley shown in Fig. 30B; they featured dome-shaped turrets and were later transferred to Chevrolet truck chassis.

30D Rolls-Royce

31A: During the thirties, Morris-Commercial Cars Ltd in England produced many military trucks, notably the 15-cwt 4 × 2 Model CS8. A variant of the CS8 was the CS9, which appeared with several styles of armoured bodywork. Illustrated is one which was converted to an armoured command vehicle, used in North Africa in 1941. (IWM photo E380)

31B: Lancia armoured cars of the early twenties, based on commercial $1\frac{1}{2}$-ton 4 × 2 truck chassis, were employed both by the RAF and by the Royal Ulster Constabulary. This is an open-top RAF type (1922); there was also a fully enclosed variant with a small turret, mounting a Lewis machine gun.

31C: A brace of Italian Army armoured cars of the thirties, abandoned in Libya in 1941. They were based on Spa $2\frac{1}{2}$-ton 4 × 2 Model 38R truck chassis, which the *Regio Esercito* used for various types of vehicles. (IWM photo E2040)

31A Morris-Commercial

31B Lancia

31C Spa

## THE INTER-WAR YEARS

32A Dutch Armoured Cars

32B : AB Landsverk in Sweden produced various types of armoured cars which were commercially available. In the foreground of this photograph, taken in 1933 in the Landsverk works, is the hull for the chassis shown on the right—a modified Ford V8 with semi-solid tyres, duplicate driving controls at the rear and an additional forward/reverse gearbox. The resulting vehicle was designated Landsverk 185.

32A : Among the few armoured cars used by the Netherlands Army (originally by the Amsterdam Police) were these three improvised vehicles, based on commercial 4 × 2 truck chassis. They carried the names 'Bison', 'Wisent' and 'Buffel', and were made in Haarlem.

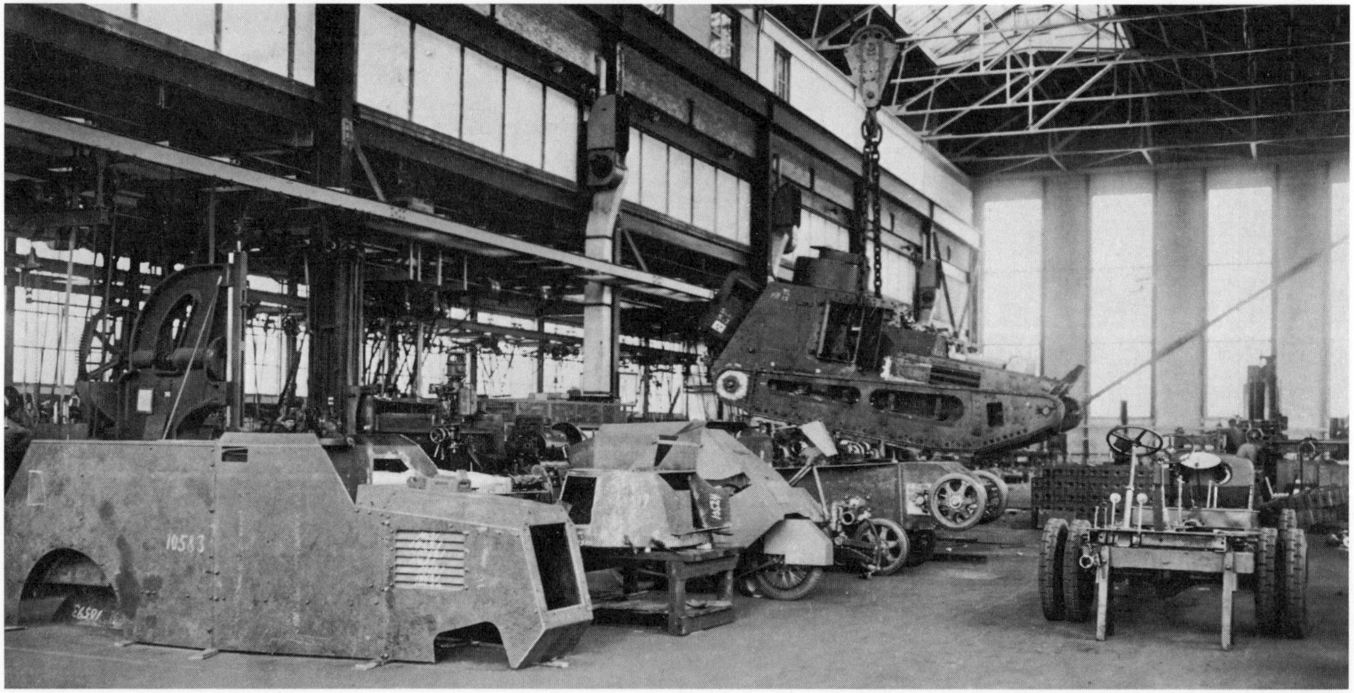

32B Landsverk

33A Pontiac

33B Oldsmobile

33C Ford

33A: During the late twenties and early thirties the US Army experimented with various types of armoured cars based on contemporary passenger car chassis. Armour ranged from radiator and windshield protection to fully armoured hulls, the latter exemplified by this Pontiac-based unit.

33B: A 1932 Oldsmobile Phaeton, provided with radiator and windshield armour protection. Similar vehicles appeared on Pontiac, Willys and other car chassis. There was a machine gun mounting on the right-hand side of the windshield armour.

33C: Two armoured cars and a string of desert patrol vehicles, all based on 1938 American Ford V8 4 × 2 truck chassis. They were in service with the Arab Legion in what is now Jordan. (IWM photo E346)

# THE INTER-WAR YEARS

34A Skoda

34A: In addition to 4 × 2 conventional rear-wheel drive (4 × 2) armoured cars, various purpose-built four-wheel drive (4 × 4) armoured cars were developed in several countries. This is a Czech Skoda PA3, *Vzor 27*, successor of the PA1 (1923) and PA2 (1925). It was of almost symmetrical layout and 24 were made during 1926–27. The engine was 60-bhp 4-cyl. Skoda of 5·68 litres and all four wheels could be steered by either the front or rear driver. Maximum speed was 35 km/h in either direction.

34B Berliet

34B: Berliet in France produced several types of all-wheel drive armoured cars. Dated 7 January 1930, this photograph shows a Model VUDB 4 × 4 prototype, 50 of which were subsequently supplied to the French and 12 to the Belgians. They were manufactured at Berliet's Montplaisier works.

34C Panhard

34C: One of the most numerous French 4 × 4 armoured cars of the mid-thirties was the Panhard 178, known officially as the *Auto-Mitrailleuse de Découverte 1935* (AMD 1935). It had a 115-bhp 4-cyl. rear-mounted engine and a maximum speed of 75–80 km/h.

35A: In 1921 Daimler in Germany produced 31 large armoured cars for police use. They were known as *Schupo-Sonderwagen* and had front and rear steering as shown in this $\frac{3}{4}$-rear view of the running chassis. Benz and Ehrhardt built similar vehicles, also with four-wheel drive.

35B: Based on a First World War Ehrhardt four-wheel drive chassis was this armoured car of the Netherlands Army. The original armoured hull had been substituted by a Dutch one, made by Siderius of Utrecht. The rear driving controls were retained.

35A Daimler

35B Ehrhardt

35C/D: In 1934/35 the German *Wehrmacht* developed a new 4 × 4 armoured car, which remained in production until 1942. The chassis was made by Auto-Union's Horch division and was basically similar to that of the military standardized heavy passenger car, the main difference being the rear mounting of the engine. Shown are a test chassis and a completed vehicle (*see* also page 61).

35C Auto-Union/Horch

35D Auto-Union/Horch

## THE INTER-WAR YEARS

36A Straussler

36B Straussler

36C Straussler

36D Straussler

36A: Pioneer of the modern four-wheel drive rear-engined armoured car with independent suspension was Nicholas Straussler, a British consulting engineer of Hungarian origin. Designed in 1932/33, the prototype chassis (shown) was built by Manfred Weiss in Budapest. It was known as the AC1 and had four-wheel steering. The engine was an OHV 4-cyl. of 100 bhp at 3500 rpm, driving through a 4-speed gearbox. Fitted with a sheet metal mock-up body it was tested by the British War Office in 1933.
36B: The Straussler AC1 chassis was later fitted with a mock-up wooden body which became the prototype for the later Alvis-Straussler AC3 production model (*qv*).
36C/D: Meanwhile Straussler had designed an improved chassis, known as the AC2. This had duplicate driving controls at the rear and other modifications and was driven from Budapest, where it was made, to London with the temporary bodywork shown.

36E: Fitted with an—easily removable—mild steel hull the Straussler AC2 was tested by the British Air Ministry (RAF) in the Middle East. The tests included an overland journey from Port Said to Baghdad.

36E Straussler

37A Alvis-Straussler

37A: Straussler reached an agreement with Alvis of Coventry for series production of his armoured car design. Under the name Alvis-Straussler Ltd a number of them were produced, powered by a 120-bhp 4·3-litre 6-cyl. Alvis engine and designated AC3 (or ACIII). Twelve cars were supplied to the Netherlands East Indies, in 1938/39; one of these is shown (Model AC3D).

37B Alvis-Straussler

37B: One of three Alvis-Straussler armoured cars delivered to the Portuguese Army in 1937/38. They were similar to the AC3D. Manfred Weiss in Hungary, makers of the original chassis, produced about 125 units, known as 39M Csaba, for the Hungarian Army and for export (probably including Japan).

37C Alvis-Straussler

37C: The RAF acquired 12 'Cars, Armoured, Alvis-Straussler, Type A', mainly for service in the Middle East. They differed from the AC3D in having vertical hull sides, 10·50–20 instead of 9·00–22 tyres, and various minor details.

37D Straussler

37D: Straussler had also developed some unusual 4 × 4 tractors of which the front and rear halves pivoted in the horizontal plane, enabling the four wheels always to remain on the ground. At least one prototype armoured car was made using a chassis of this configuration. The engine was at the rear.

## THE INTER-WAR YEARS

38A Morris-Commercial

38A: In 1938 the British War Office conducted tests with several types of armoured cars, including a rear-engined Morris. This had a backbone chassis with the wheels suspended independently at the ends of diagonally placed swinging arms, which also contained the drive shafts. Its very unorthodox design utilized no universal joints and was the subject of various patents (Nos. 480969, 481005/6/9) in the name of P. G. Rose and Morris-Commercial Cars Ltd. Designated Model Q, the chassis also appeared in front-engined form, for use as an artillery tractor. The engine was a 6-cyl. Model VEB of 3745-cc, developing 80–85 bhp. The vehicles never reached quantity production.

38B Landsverk

38C Pavesi

38B: Another interesting rear-engined armoured car chassis was this experimental Swedish Landsverk fm/29 (1929) with front and rear driving positions and stub axle-mounted anti-bellying spare wheels.

38C: The Italian Pavesi 4 × 4 articulated tractor chassis was used for several armoured vehicles exemplified by this L140 model of 1926. It carried a crew of four and three machine guns. The wheels were of 1·20-m diameter.

38D: This Italian *Autoprotetto S37* was an armoured truck for use in the desert. It was based on the standardized Italian Army Spa AS37 4 × 4 truck, of which there were several derivatives, including the TL37 artillery tractor.

38D Spa

39A Marmon-Herrington

39A: The well-known American firm of Marmon-Herrington in Indianapolis, Indiana, from 1934 produced a range of armoured vehicles, all of the four-wheel drive configuration and available commercially. One of their first clients was the Iranian (Persian) Army, who, in 1934, took delivery of this Model A7 Scout Car, as well as a fleet of armoured cars.

39B: Another early Marmon-Herrington combat vehicle was this armoured car, equipped for steering from either end. It had a 221 CID Ford V8 engine as standard with four-speed gearbox and two-speed transfer (4FIR × 2); lowest possible overall gear reduction was 165:1.

39B Marmon-Herrington

39C White Indiana

39C: The US Army Ordnance Department developed a long range of armoured scout cars throughout the thirties, culminating in the well-known Scout Car, M3A1 (*see* 59A). This is the M1 (originally T7) of 1934/35, which was based on a White Indiana Model 12X4 4 × 4 chassis.

40A Tatra

40A: Six-wheeled armoured cars began to appear in the late twenties and both 6 × 4 and 6 × 6 designs were made in several countries. Shown is a line-up of Czechoslovakian Tatras, designated *vzor 30* and produced in 1932 on the contemporary Tatra T72 $1\frac{1}{2}$-ton 6 × 4 truck chassis. Powered by an air-cooled horizontally-opposed four-cylinder engine of 1910 cc the vehicle featured a tubular backbone chassis with independent rear suspension by means of swinging half axles.

40B: Berliet of France, in addition to 4 × 4 types, launched some 6 × 6 models, including the VPRM with equally-spaced axles. This is the prototype, which made its debut in Algeria in 1930. Note the dual tyres on the centre axle. Steering was on the fore- and rearmost wheels.

40C: This Berliet 6 × 6, Model UDB4, first appeared in 1934 and was powered by an 80-bhp 5-litre 6-cyl. engine, driving through a six forward and reverse transmission. Maximum speed: forward 60 km/h, rearward 55 km/h. The brakes acted on the centre wheels and the transmission.

40C Berliet

40D: The French Army used many vehicles based on six-wheel drive Laffly chassis of the late thirties, including various armoured types. This 5-ton *Auto-Mitrailleuse* had 5–12-mm armour and a 13·2-mm turret-mounted gun. Note the front bumper wheels.

40B Berliet

40D Laffly

41A: In the late twenties some German manufacturers introduced light six-wheeled (6 × 4) truck chassis for commercial and military purposes and in 1929 the German military authorities began preparations for the development of armoured cars on modified versions of these chassis (Büssing-NAG, Daimler-Benz, Magirus). One modification was the provision of duplicate driving controls at the rear. Eventually a relatively large number of these armoured cars were made, in three main versions: *Sd.Kfz.231* (basic model), *232* (with radio) and *263* (command, with radio and fixed turret). Shown is a pilot model of the *Sd.Kfz.232* with early type aerial.

41A *Sd.Kfz.232*

41B: *Sd.Kfz.231* production model on Büssing-NAG chassis, 1934–35. It had a 4·5-litre 70-bhp 6-cyl. engine with 4F1R × 2 transmission, driving the tandem rear axles.

41C: *Sd.Kfz.232* radio-equipped armoured cars entering Prague in the spring of 1939. Note the typical German overhead type aerials.

41B *Sd.Kfz.231*

41C *Sd.Kfz.232*

## THE INTER-WAR YEARS

42A: The British also developed several six-wheeled armoured cars, beginning in the late twenties. This is an experimental vehicle, produced by Vickers-Armstrongs on a Crossley 6 × 4 light truck chassis in 1929/30.

42B: Crossley/Vickers armoured car on 30/70 HP 6 × 4 medium truck chassis with 70-bhp 4-cyl. engine, used by the RAF in the Middle East. Note the dome-shaped turret, which was reminiscent of the Indian Pattern armoured cars (*see* page 30 and Fig. 42C) and featured four alternative mountings for Vickers machine guns (normally two were carried). This vehicle weighed just over seven tons and could attain 50 mph.

42A Crossley

42C: In 1928 Guy Motors of Wolverhampton supplied a number of 9-ton armoured cars for service in India. Their 120-bhp 6-cyl. engine provided a top speed of 45 mph. The official designation was 'Armoured Car, Guy, Indian Pattern'.

42B Crossley

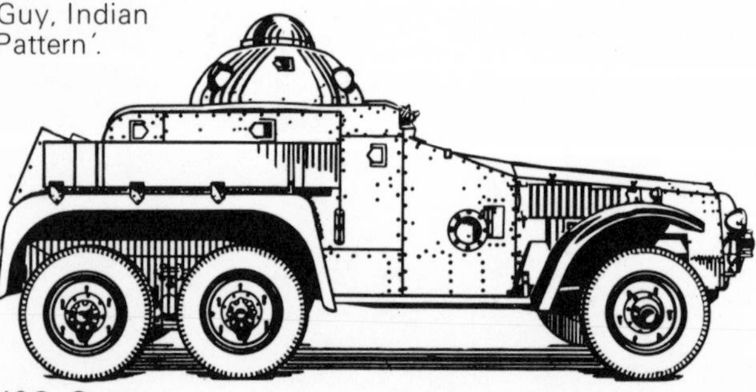

42C Guy

42D: The Lanchester Motor Co. were the first manufacturers to produce 6 × 4 armoured cars in quantity for the British Army, the first prototypes being ordered in 1927. Shown is a Mark I, 18 of which were made (followed by 17 of later types). Like Daimler, Lanchester was a member of the BSA Group of Companies.

# THE BIRMINGHAM SMALL ARMS Co., Ltd.

*A Great Engineering Combine Controlling These Famous Firms :-*

| | |
|---|---|
| **Daimler** COVENTRY. | Makers of Daimler Cars and Motor Buses. Great War production included Aeroplanes, Aero Engines, Tank Engine and Transmission Units, Tractors, Lorries, Staff Cars, Ambulances and Shells. |
| **Lanchester** COVENTRY. | Makers of Lanchester Cars and Armoured Car chassis. Great War production included Armoured Cars, Staff Cars, Aero Engines, Kite Balloon Winches and Paravanes. |
| **B.S.A Cycles** BIRMINGHAM. | Makers of B.S.A. Bicycles, Motor Cycles and small Cars. Great War production included Military Bicycles and Motor Cycles, Aero Engine Components and Shells. |
| **B.S.A. Guns** BIRMINGHAM. | Makers of Sporting and Military Small Arms of all types, and of machine guns. Great War production included 1,600,000 Rifles and 146,000 Lewis Guns. |
| **B.S.A. Tools** BIRMINGHAM. | Makers of high-class Machine Tools and Small Tools with a wide experience in the manufacture of Special Tools and Cutters for Aero Engine production |
| **JESSOPS & SAVILLES** SHEFFIELD. | Makers of Tool Steels and Constructional Steels of all descriptions. Specialists in Crucible Tool Steels, Stainless Steel and other high-grade Alloy Steels for the Automobile and Aircraft Industries. |

*All enquiries to be addressed to The Birmingham Small Arms Co., Ltd., Birmingham, II*

42D Lanchester

43A Lanchester

43A: Chassis of the Lanchester Mark I, 1929. Unlike most contemporary 6 × 4 armoured cars, the Lanchester had a purpose-built chassis, rather than that of a truck. The engine was a 40 HP OHV Six, coupled to a transmission of the 3-speed planetary (epicyclic) type, with a 2-speed auxiliary gearbox. Worm drive was used on both rear axles and all braking was on the rear bogie. Note the dual steering wheels and the leather gaiters enveloping the long inverted leaf springs of the bogie.

43B: The Morris-Commercial D-type light 6 × 4 chassis was widely used by the British Army, with a variety of body types. Unusual was this mock-up 'tank', doubling as a gun tractor.

43B Morris-Commercial

44A FWD England

44A: Probably the first British six-wheel drive armoured car chassis was this rear-engined unit produced by the Four Wheel Drive Lorry Co. Ltd about 1929, under the name FWD England. The low forward driver's position is noteworthy. Powered by a 4-cyl. engine with eight forward and two reverse speeds this interesting design did not progress beyond the prototype testing stage.

44B Scammell

44B: Scammell Lorries Ltd of Watford designed two six-wheeled armoured car chassis, also in the late twenties. This is a scale model of about 1928, based on the design of the then recently introduced Pioneer cross-country vehicle. It had independent front suspension on a centrally-pivoted front axle and the rear wheels were attached to balancing beams. The engine was a vertical radial air-cooled unit. This project did not materialize.

44C: Another experimental Scammell Pioneer-based armoured car chassis appeared in 1929; this time a full-scale model was built and tested, albeit with a mock-up body. It was considerably lower than the standard Pioneer. The complete chassis weighed just over five tons and had a wheelbase of 13 ft 6 in. It was powered by the standard Scammell 40 HP 4-cyl. 5 × $5\frac{1}{2}$-in engine which gave 53 bhp at 1000 rpm, but could be run up to 2000 rpm (max. bhp 65 approx.). The gearbox was a special 5-speed unit. (For additional coverage of these vehicles see the title *Scammell Vehicles* in this series.)

44C Scammell

45A Daimler-Benz

45B/C/D: Front, rear and right-hand side views of the Landsverk 181 as supplied to the Netherlands Army, who had 12 of these and 12 of the later V8-engined model, designated *Paw.M36* and *M38* respectively (*Paw—pantserwagen*, armoured car; 36 and 38 indicated the year of delivery). Both types had the same turret, mounting a 3·7-cm gun and one machine gun; in addition there were machine guns in the front and rear face of the hull. The vehicles could be driven in both directions at reasonable speeds and saw active service during the country's resistance to the Nazi invasion in May 1940; surviving vehicles were later used by the Germans.

45A: AB Landsverk in Sweden produced six-wheeled armoured cars for export (the Netherlands, Ireland). The first of these appeared in 1933 and was based on virtually the same Daimler-Benz 6-cyl. 6 × 4 chassis as the Germans used for their own *Sd.Kfz.231*, etc. (*see* page 41). It was designated Landsverk 181 and usually had semi-solid tyres (with air chambers). Later a more powerful model was introduced, with a Büssing-NAG V8 engine, again of German origin.

45B Landsverk

45C Landsverk

45D Landsverk

## THE INTER-WAR YEARS

46A Dutch 'Buffel' Armoured Car

46A: At least one of the Dutch improvised armoured cars (*see* page 32) was later (1938/39) modernized and fitted with a 6 × 4 truck chassis, electric lighting, etc. The rear steering-wheel is just visible through the doorway.

46C DAF

46B: In 1938 DAF of Eindhoven in the Netherlands designed a six-wheeled armoured car, using their Trado rear bogie and a Ford V8 engine. Illustrated is a scale model of the original design.

46C: The DAF armoured car reached the production stage and 12 were made, designated *Paw.M39*. They had Landsverk turrets, the same as fitted on the *Paw.M36* (*see* previous page) and *M38*. The 95-bhp Ford V8 engine was mounted at the rear on the right, alongside the rear driver/gunner. The hull was of strikingly modern and advanced design with angled side plates and sloping glacis plates at front and rear. In addition to the 37-mm Bofors gun, three machine guns were mounted. Most of these vehicles were later used by the Germans for internal security work. No chassis was used, all components being attached directly to the hull. The cars weighed about 5800 kg and could be fitted with Philips radio communications equipment.

46B DAF

47A: Eight-wheeled armoured cars appeared in various configurations. The Germans began development of such vehicles in 1927, and experimental prototypes were built by Daimler-Benz and Magirus. In addition, Büssing-NAG produced a ten-wheeler. Testing took place in Russia, Germany being forbidden to have vehicles of this type, under the Versailles Treaty. The picture shows a Daimler-Benz prototype, clad in cork for camouflage and to improve its swimming ability—one of the requirements laid down by the military authorities.

47B: The eventual outcome of the German *Vielradwagen* programme was the Büssing-NAG rear-engined 8 × 8 chassis (*Achtradwagen*), which first appeared in 1934/35 and was subsequently produced in considerable quantity until 1942. All wheels were steered and independently sprung. Shown are a radio-equipped *Sd.Kfz.263* (*8-Rad*) (left) and a *Sd.Kfz.233*, the latter being a turret-less model with 7·5-cm gun.

47A Daimler-Benz

47C: In Austria, Steyr-Daimler-Puch AG produced a number of unusual 8 × 8 armoured cars, designated ADGZ. During 1935–37, 27 were made; in 1938, when Austria was 'annexed' by the *Third Reich*, these were taken over by the German *Wehrmacht*. An interesting feature was the vehicle's Voith hydraulic transmission with torque converter.

47B Büssing-NAG

47C Austro-Daimler

## THE BLITZKRIEG ERA

**In 1939 it started—the 'lightning war', better known in the German terminology as the *Blitzkrieg*. It was the period of the rapid German armoured advances, first into Poland, then Denmark, the Low Countries, France. . . .**

**By the end of 1941 practically the whole world was involved in the Second World War. Armoured wheeled vehicles used in the early stages of this conflict were of a large variety; not until about 1942/43 was it possible to phase out and replace the makeshift and little-tried new types—as well as antiquated pre-war machines.**

48A Ford/Marmon-Herrington

48B Ford/Marmon-Herrington

48A/B: The Belgian Army, conquered in mid-1940, employed a variety of vehicles based on Ford/Marmon-Herrington 4 × 4 chassis, including a fleet of these armoured anti-tank gun tractors. The chassis were assembled in Antwerp from American components; the armoured hulls were made by Usines Ragheno of Malines (Mechelen). The *Wehrmacht* later used at least one of these vehicles as a command car.

48C Panhard

48D Panhard

48C/D: French Panhard 178 armoured cars were captured by the Germans in considerable quantity and some 150 were taken into German service as *Panzerspähwagen P204(f)*. Shown are one of the *SS* and one of the *Wehrmacht*, the latter being one of about 40 converted for running on railroads on the Eastern Front. The overhead radio aerial was also a German modification.

## THE BLITZKRIEG ERA

49A Bedford 'Armadillo'

49C Leyland 'Beaver-Eel'

49C: The 'Beaver-Eel' was named after Lord Beaverbrook—then Minister of Aircraft Production—and designed for the defence of aircraft factories. Several hundred were made—this one by the London, Midland and Scottish (LMS) Railway workshops at Wolverton. The vehicles were based on 6 × 4 Leyland Retriever chassis and later converted back to 3-ton GS trucks.

49B 'Bison'

49A: Great Britain, expecting a German invasion at any time, prepared herself and came up with an unbelievable assortment of improvised armoured vehicles for Home Defence. This mobile pill-box, one of several hundreds known as 'Armadillos', was based on a commercial Bedford platform truck. The armour consisted of a double-skin timber box, the space between outer and inner skin filled with small pebbles.

49B: Named 'Bisons', after the trade-mark of the London firm of Concrete Ltd who made them, were these mobile blockhouses which appeared on various makes and types of heavy commercial trucks. Their concrete armour was proof against AP (armour-piercing) bullets.

49D: This Morris-based wooden 'armoured car' was intended for protection of airfields. It is unknown whether it was seriously intended as a prototype or merely acted to frighten possible *Fallschirmjäger* (German parachutists). The turret side door is shown fully open.

49D Morris

## THE BLITZKRIEG ERA

50A Fordson/Campbell

50A: In 1940, Mr Leo Villa, racing mechanic of Sir Malcolm Campbell, at the latter's instigation built this armoured tractor, based on a paraffin-engined Fordson Major. The steering-wheel was repositioned to the right and the engine could be crank-started inside the hull. In addition to the driver, there was standing space for a Bren-gunner, who turned the turret with his shoulders.

50B: The Campbell armoured tractor prototype was turned over to Briggs Motor Bodies Ltd at Dagenham who reproduced the hull in real armour plate. After testing at Farnborough the machine was rejected.

50C: Another, more successful, Campbell/Villa project was a Fordson truck-based armoured car. Again a mild-steel prototype was made, which went to Briggs for the manufacture of a pilot model in $\frac{7}{8}$- or 1-in armour-plate. The photo shows Mr Leo Villa in the prototype.

50D: The Briggs-built pilot model of the Campbell/Villa armoured car was built on the same Fordson V8 chassis but in addition to having real armour featured several other modifications, including double-hinged full-width hull roof hatches. This vehicle led to the production of some 70 similar but further improved armoured cars on Dodge Kew truck chassis.

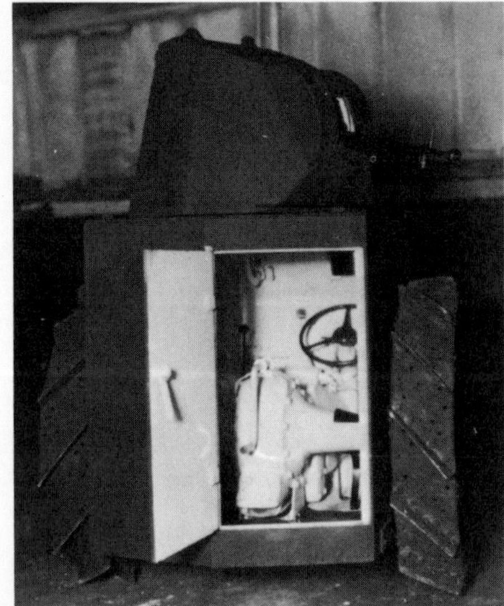

50B Fordson/Campbell

50C Fordson/Campbell

50D Fordson/Campbell

51A: A very popular British armoured vehicle was the Daimler (originally BSA) scout car which later became generally known as the Daimler 'Dingo'. Of rear-engined all-wheel drive design it had an octagon-shaped hull for a crew of two and steered on all wheels. Shown is one of the early production models with German *Wehrmacht* number plate: this vehicle was one of a number the British had left behind in their evacuation from Dunkirk. The Germans used these under the designation *leichter Panzerspähwagen Mk I 202 (e)*.
51B: Scout Car Daimler Mark IA at Aberdeen Proving Ground in the USA in February 1942. The picture clearly shows the rear wheel steering mechanism.

51A Daimler

51B Daimler

51C Humber

51C: Light Reconnaissance Car Humber Mark II was built on a modified Humber Super Snipe car chassis and unlike its predecessor (Humber Mark I, Ironside I) featured a small turret. This chassis was used for a variety of military vehicles, including saloon cars and light trucks.

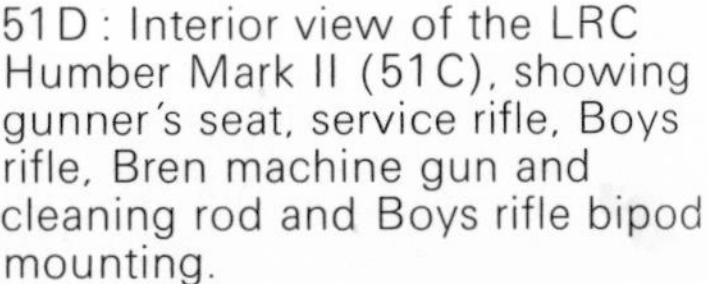

51D: Interior view of the LRC Humber Mark II (51C), showing gunner's seat, service rifle, Boys rifle, Bren machine gun and cleaning rod and Boys rifle bipod mounting.

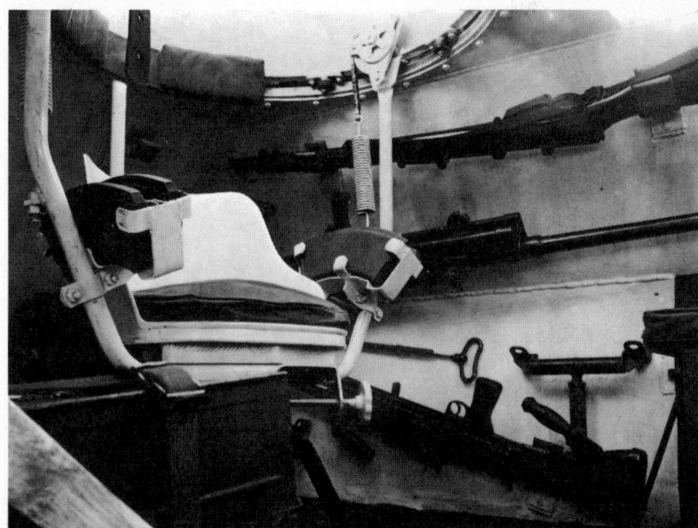

51D Humber

## THE BLITZKRIEG ERA

52A : Among the many odd-looking armoured cars built in Britain after the outbreak of war were the Standard 'Beaverettes'. They were made originally at the instigation of Lord Beaverbrook, chiefly for the defence of aircraft factories. They were of two main types : the improvised Marks I and II (shown) on a conventional Standard 14 HP car chassis and the fully-enclosed boxy Marks III and IV. They were used both by the Army and the RAF.

52A Standard 'Beaverette'

52B Standard 'Beaverette'

52B : Compared with 'Beaverettes' Mark I and II, the Mark III and IV looked even more peculiar. They had a fully-enclosed hull on a very short (74-in wheelbase) Standard car chassis with big tyres, size 9·00-13. Shown are a pair of Mark IIIs of an Army Recce Battalion on exercise in Northern Ireland in October 1941. (IWM photo H14875)

52C : The 'Beaverette' Mark IV had a stepped-back hull front but was generally similar to the Mark III. This is probably the only one of its type left, restored and preserved by a private collector in England.

52C Standard 'Beaverette'

53A Morris

53B Morris

53A: Morris also produced a variety of armoured cars, before settling down on the production of one final type—the rear-engined 'Car, 4 × 4, Light Reconnaissance, Morris Mark II'. Illustrated on the left is the original (Mark I) version of the latter; this was a 4 × 2 vehicle with coil-spring independent front suspension. On the right is an experimental armoured car—a small single-seater with two fixed machine guns in the front glacis plate, aimed with the car itself. It was known as the 'Glanville Fighter Car'.

53B: One of the prototypes of the Morris Light Reconnaissance Car. The total production of the later Marks I (*see* 53A) and II amounted to some 2200 units. Note the camouflage patterns on the factory walls.

53C: The Morris 'Salamander' was an experimental two-man model, appearing only in prototype form and intended to replace the unarmoured Bren gun-equipped motorcycle/sidecar combinations of the period. (Hillman developed a similar model, called the 'Gnat'). This artist's impression of 1942 shows 'Salamanders' with proposed floating pontoons, enabling them to cross inland waterways.

53C Morris 'Salamander'

# THE BLITZKRIEG ERA

54A/B: In addition to scout cars (*see* page 51) the Daimler Motor Co. produced several thousand armoured cars. The rear-mounted 95-bhp 6-cyl. engine drove through a fluid flywheel with 5-speed (forward and reverse) pre-selector transmission. Final drive was via four individual propeller shafts to all wheels. These Daimlers entered service in 1941.

54A Daimler

54B Daimler

54C Guy

54C: Guy Motors developed an armoured car—initially known as 'Tank, Light, Wheeled Mark I'—based on a rear-engined variant of their Quad-Ant 4 × 4 military chassis. Five prototypes were built in 1938, using mild steel hulls. Production models had welded hulls and turrets, employing a welding process specially developed by the company.

55A Guy

55A: Batch of Guy armoured cars leaving the company's Fallings Park, Wolverhampton, works. Just visible in the background are two Quad-Ant artillery tractors—a production model and the prototype with wooden test body. Owing to heavy production commitments for other Guy military vehicles, production of armoured cars was turned over to the Karrier division of the Rootes Group, although Guy Motors continued manufacturing the hulls.

55B Humber

55C Humber

55B: Karrier Motors produced the armoured cars, developed by Guy (*see* 54C and 55A), under the name Humber—in order to avoid possible confusion with the ubiquitous Bren/ Universal Carrier (*see* 57A). This is an 'Armoured Car, Humber, Mark I', armed with two turret-mounted machine guns, a 15- and a 7·92-mm Besa. Distinguishing exterior differences compared with the Guy were the long telescopic front shock absorbers and the horizontal rear wing tops. The engine was a Rootes 6-cyl. (Guy used a Meadows 4-cyl.).

55C: Armoured Car, Humber, Mark II featured hull modifications at the front and the rear. The solid rear plate was replaced by a louvred pattern to improve engine cooling.

56A/B: Guy Motors also made 21 armoured command vehicles (ACV), based on their four-wheel drive Gardner diesel-engined Lizard chassis. They were issued to formation headquarters in the UK and North Africa.

56C: The British Army's standard ACV was this fully-armoured edition of the AEC Matador, which appeared in several variants. Even Field-Marshal Rommel used one of these (captured) vehicles in the Libyan campaigns. Like the Guy Lizard it had a diesel engine and a side tent extension.

56A Guy

56B Guy

56D: Vauxhall Motors produced large numbers of Bedford 4 × 2 and 4 × 4 military trucks and this 'Lorry, 30-cwt, 4 × 2, Armoured Anti-Tank, Bedford' appeared in 1940, designated Model OXA. In total, 950 were ordered. They were improvised vehicles, used mainly by home defence mobile divisions. Most were later reconverted to GS trucks.

56C AEC

56D Bedford

57A Guy

57A: The British tracked Universal Carrier was built in large numbers by several manufacturers in the UK as well as in Canada and—in modified form—in the USA. Shown are a standard 'Carrier, Universal, No. 1, Mk I' (right) and a wheeled version which was ordered from Guy Motors in late 1939. It was based on the rear-engined Guy armoured car chassis but appeared only in mild steel prototype form.

57B: Some 4-in Naval guns were mounted on Foden DG/6/10 10-ton 6 × 4 military truck chassis with open-top armoured cabs. One is shown during exercises in the UK, in August 1941. (IWM photo H12692)

57C: The 'Basilisk' flame-thrower was a conversion of an AEC Armoured Car, which had been launched in 1941 as a private venture. The armoured cars—based on a rear-engined version of the AEC Matador 4 × 4 chassis—were produced in quantity but the 'Basilisk' remained a prototype.

57C AEC 'Basilisk'

57B Foden

57D: Another flamethrower was the 'Cockatrice', based on the Bedford QL 3-ton 4 × 4 chassis. Sixty were supplied to the Royal Navy for airfield defence. As on the 'Basilisk' (57C) the flame projector was mounted in a small turret.

57D Bedford 'Cockatrice'

58A Ford/Marmon-Herrington

58B Ford/Marmon-Herrington

58A: The Australians in 1940/41 produced these front-engined scout cars, known officially as 'Cars, Scout (Aust.), Dingo'. They were based on converted Ford truck chassis, shortened to 110-in. wheelbase and provided with Marmon-Herrington front wheel drive and 2-speed auxiliary gearbox.
58B: Other Australian types included the 'Cars, Armoured (Aust.) No. 2, Curlew', again on a short Ford/Marmon-Herrington 4 × 4 chassis (earlier edition had 4 × 2 drive). They had a door on each side and at the rear. The picture was taken in Sydney in May 1941.

58C Ford/Marmon-Herrington

58C: South Africa produced an impressive range of Ford-based armoured cars, mostly (i.e. except the 1940 Mark I) incorporating Marmon-Herrington front wheel drive. Illustrated are Mark IIIs, some 2630 of which were built in 1941/42. These, and other Marks, were widely used by the South African and British forces, as well as several allies. Later models were rear-engined.
58D/E: India also assembled a large number of military vehicles, mainly from Canadian Ford and GM components. Some were entirely different from those which the Canadians produced themselves, particularly the 'Carriers, Wheeled, Indian Pattern' of which the limited-production Mark I edition is shown. It was a $113\frac{1}{2}$-in wheelbase 4 × 4 Ford-based front-engined car; later Marks were built in large quantities on special Ford rear-engined 101-in wheelbase Canadian Military Pattern chassis.

58D Ford/Marmon-Herrington

58E Ford/Marmon-Herrington

59A: The final model in the range of US Army scout cars, developed during the thirties, was the Car, Scout, 4 × 4, M3A1. Built in considerable quantities by the White Motor Co. of Cleveland, Ohio, its purpose was officially summed up in the words 'to provide mobility and crew protection for reconnaissance in combat'. Many of these vehicles were later also supplied—under the Lend-Lease agreement—to Britain, Canada, Russia and other allies.

59B: This armour-clad truck, described as an 'Armored Riot Squad Car', was a commercial offering by Smart Engineering Corp. in the USA. It was based on a 1940 Ford V8 truck chassis.

59C: In 1941 the US Army tested this scout car on the contemporary military standard $\frac{1}{2}$-ton 4 × 4 truck chassis—the Dodge T211. It was a private venture by the Chrysler Corp. and did not progress beyond the prototype stage.

59D: Another non-starter was this armoured O.P. (Observation Post) Tender, offered by the Ford Motor Co. to the US Artillery. It was one of several experimental 4 × 4 vehicles produced by Ford in 1941/42. Following tests at Aberdeen Proving Ground in 1942, this vehicle was rejected and subsequently used as a runabout. The officer on the left is Colonel Robert J. Icks—then in charge of automotive testing at APG. Colonel Icks, now retired, is and was one of the world's leading and most respected authors/historians on the subject of armoured fighting vehicles.

59B Ford

59C Dodge

59A White

59D Ford

60A GAZ BA20

60B GAZ BA10

60A: The Soviet Union during the thirties had developed two main types of armoured cars: four-wheelers based on the GAZ-M-1 passenger car chassis and six-wheelers based on the GAZ-AAA 6 × 4 truck chassis. Of both types there were several variants and modifications. Both were powered by a GAZ M1 4-cyl. side-valve engine of 50 bhp at 2800 rpm, which was similar to the American Ford Model B engine (GAZ cars and trucks were patterned on US Fords). Illustrated is the four-wheeled BA20 in its standard form and—in the centre—with frame aerial around the hull.

60B: The Soviet six-wheeled armoured car BA10, a 5-ton vehicle with a turret-mounted 45-mm gun. This illustration is of German origin and shows the vehicle minus its headlights and the stub-axle-mounted spare wheels, which were located to the rear of the front wheels (the bracket is just visible). The *Wehrmacht* in 1941 captured large numbers of these armoured cars and used the serviceable ones under the designation *Panzerspähwagen BAF 203(r)*.

60C GAZ BA10

60C: During the Russian invasion into Finland (1939/40), as well as the German invasion into Russia (1941), countless armoured cars were abandoned—usually after having been destroyed by their crews. This picture was taken on the Finnish front, at a point on the Karelian isthmus (the land bridge connecting Russia and Finland, between the Gulf of Finland and Lake Ladoga).

61A: The *Wehrmacht* in their *Blitzkrieg* used three basic types of armoured cars: 4 × 4, 6 × 4 and 8 × 8. Of each there were several variants. Shown are some 4 × 4 units coming up along a railway track. The leading vehicles are a *Sd.Kfz.221* (with machine gun) and a *Sd.Kfz.222* (with 2-cm gun).

61A Auto-Union/Horch

61B: The *Sd.Kfz.221* armoured car and variants were based on the Auto-Union *Einheitsfahrgestell I für s. Pkw* (universal chassis I for heavy cars), which had a Horch V8 engine at the rear (3·5-litre during 1935–40, then 3·8-litre until 1942; these two versions—types A and B—had mechanical and hydraulic brakes respectively). Shown is an early type. They featured independent suspension and optional four-wheel steering.

61B Auto-Union/Horch

61C Auto-Union/Horch

61C: *Sd.Kfz.221* (4 × 4) and *Sd.Kfz.232* (8 × 8) in Holland during the German invasion in May 1940.

61D: One of the few remaining German armoured cars of Second World War-vintage, resting in a barn in Wiltshire, England.

61D Auto-Union/Horch

62A Fiat/Spa

62B. Lancia

62B/C: Unusual and yet familiar-looking, was the Italian *Lince*. This was a 'Chinese copy' of the early four-wheel steer British Daimler Scout Car (*see* page 51) the main difference being the power unit: an 8-cyl. Lancia Astura. Date and quantity are uncertain, but it would appear that between 150 and 250 were built between 1940 and 1944. It is not unlikely that they were reworked captured British vehicles. The car shown in Fig. 62B is exhibited in the Military Transport Museum in Rome.

62A: Most interesting of the Italian Army armoured cars were the Fiat/Spa *Autoblinda* AB40 and 41 (later succeeded by the AB43). The rear-mounted 6-cyl. 5-litre engine drove all four wheels via individual propeller shafts, from a central lockable differential. The AB40 carried three 8-mm Breda machine guns—two in the turret, one at the rear. On the AB41 (shown) the former were replaced by a 20-mm gun. They were sophisticated and complicated vehicles but well-built. There were also some open-top variants, including the *Camionetta 43 Sahariana*—a desert patrol/reconnaissance vehicle.

62C Lancia

63A: Italian prototype *Carro protetto trasporto truppa*, an armoured troop carrier based on the 3-ton 4 × 2 Fiat 626 truck chassis. This chassis was widely used by the Italian armed forces, both with petrol and diesel engine and with various body types.

63B: Fiat truck with armour-clad cab, found abandoned by British soldiers during the Libyan campaign. (IWM photo E1805) Later a proper armoured truck appeared, known as *Autocarro pesante Fiat 665NM blindato* (armoured heavy truck, Fiat Model 665NM). Like most Italian military vehicles it had right-hand drive, hence the extra vision slot in the windscreen armour.

63B Fiat

63C: The Japanese Imperial Army used a variety of six-wheeled (6 × 4) armoured cars, many of which could be converted for running on railroads. Illustrated is a TGE Chiyoda in 1940.

63A Fiat

63C TGE Chiyoda

# INDEX



## ACKNOWLEDGEMENTS


This book was compiled and written largely from historic source material in the library/collection of the Editor, and in addition photographs were kindly provided by Col. Robert J. Icks; Aimé van Ingelgom; Stanley C. Poole; F. T. Snyder Jr; Walter Spielberger; Leo Villa, OBE; T.Col. David Virdis; Fred Vos; B. T. White; Laurie A. Wright; as well as the following official bodies: Archivo General de la Nacion (Argentina); E. C. Armée (France); HKKL Sectie Krijgsgeschiedenis (Netherlands); the Imperial War Museum (whose reference numbers appear where applicable); and the Public Archives/National Museums of Canada.